SIMPLE ETIQUETTE IN
CHINA

ILLUSTRATED BY
IRENE SANDERSON

SIMPLE ETIQUETTE IN
CHINA

By
Caroline Mason

Paul Norbury Publications
Sandgate, Folkestone, Kent, England

SIMPLE ETIQUETTE IN CHINA

Paul Norbury Publications
Knoll House, 35 The Crescent, Sandgate,
Folkestone, Kent, England CT20 3EE

First published 1989
© Paul Norbury Publications

ISBN 0-903304-70-6

British Library Cataloguing in Publication Data
Mason, Caroline, *1949-*
   Simple etiquette in China.
   1. China. Etiquette
   I. Title
   395'.0951
   ISBN 0-904404-70-6

Set in Souvenir 11 on 12 pt by Visual Typesetting
Printed in England by BPCC Wheatons Ltd., Exeter

Contents

Introduction 7

1 The Foreigner in China 9

2 Hotels & Living Conditions 11

3 Money, Sightseeing, Tipping &
Taxis 14

4 Presents & Shopping 17

5 Conversation & Communication 19

6 Making Friends 22

7 Women Visiting China 25

8 Visiting a Doctor 27

9 Business 28

10 Banquets & Being Entertained 32

11 Alcohol & Tea 36

12 Eating Out 39

13 Japan & Hong Kong 40

14 Something About the Language 42

ACKNOWLEDGEMENTS

The author is indebted to her colleagues at the School of Oriental Studies, University of Durham, for their suggestions and comments on the original draft of this book, and is also very grateful for the discussions with Katherine Duxbury of the Sino-British Trade Council, Liz Roberts and Sue Bishop, among others.

Introduction

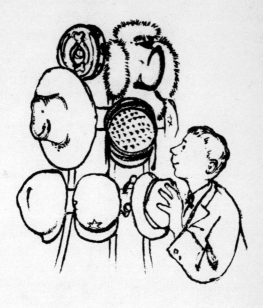

In traditional China, great importance was attached to correct behaviour within society and one of the earliest classics of Confucianism was a collection of writings on the complex details of what is translated variously as 'ceremonial,' propriety,' or 'the rites.' Today, fortunately, ideas about correct social behaviour are much simpler: they have had to change, as Chinese society has changed, and although attention is still paid to etiquette, this is by now of the kind with which foreigners can at least attempt to become familiar. This book aims to present some aspects of Chinese etiquette which it would be most useful for non-Chinese people to understand when they go to China.

Most of what is said in the following pages applies to both the People's Republic of China (PRC) *and* Taiwan. Where it applies to one and not the other, I shall make this clear. But it should be borne in mind that since the People's Republic covers a vast area, there are numerous regional differences in every field. However, it is clearly beyond the scope of this book to detail them all.

I would also like to point out that although most of the people you are likely to come into contact with will be of the Han race (i.e. what we in the West usually think of as 'Chinese'), there are over fifty minority nationalities in the PRC, totalling some six per cent of the population. These include Tibetans, Uighurs, Kazakhs, Yao, Miao, Yi and Dai.

In Taiwan, too, there are non-Han aboriginal people, and the Han Chinese fall into two fairly distinct categories of 1) Taiwanese Chinese and 2) Chinese from all parts of mainland China who went (or whose families went) to Taiwan in 1949, when the Communists took control of the Mainland. The Chinese are not such a homogeneous nation as is popularly believed in the West.

CAROLINE MASON

1

The Foreigner in China

As a foreigner in China, it is unlikely that you will ever be taken for a Chinese, and therefore allowances will be made for you. It is nevertheless a good idea to watch what Chinese people do in certain social and business situations and to try and behave in a way not incompatible with this. Your efforts will be appreciated.

The Chinese are very keen not to be seen to 'lose face' and this explains many of their behaviour patterns. Laughter, for instance, does not necessarily mean that the person laughing finds something funny (although it may, of course, mean just that): it might well be used to cover up embarrassment in an awkward situation.

Equally, a foreigner loses face by becoming angry or upset. Impatience is seen by the Chinese as a serious character flaw. In the PRC, there is an immense amount of 'red tape' involved in what to us might seem the simplest of procedures — buying train or plane tickets, for example — and it is helpful if one can learn to accept such inconveniences gracefully.

On meeting someone in China, the usual practice is to shake hands, often for a much longer time than in the West. This may be accompanied by a respectful nod. If you are being introduced to a group of people, make sure to shake hands with all of them. From then on, as far as physical contact is concerned, take your cue from the person you are talking to.

If you are with someone of the opposite sex there is unlikely to be any touching — but members of the same sex do tend to touch each other rather more than in the West. When talking, men, in particular, often stand closer to each other than they would in the West, and women frequently emphasise a point by patting each other on the arm. In some places away from large urban centres you may well see young people of the same sex walking along the street hand in hand: in Chinese society this is just an expression of friendship.

Chinese people rise early and retire early, so lunch will probably be at noon and banquets in the evening are likely to begin at six. Once the meal is over, the visitors may chat for a few minutes but should then get up and go. There is no prolonged after-dinner coffee-drinking so common in the West, and departure soon after the end of the meal is the rule in China.

2

Hotels & Living Conditions

Most visitors to China are likely to be staying in hotels. In the bigger cities — in both the PRC and Taiwan — there are numerous very modern hotels where standards of comfort are easily on a par with many top hotels in the West, but outside these cities standards can vary considerably.

In the PRC, the most comfortable (and most expensive) hotels are usually the the Joint Venture hotels, built with large injections of foreign capital and managed, generally speaking, either by westerners or Hong Kong Chinese. Also first-class are the top Chinese hotels, but service here can be a bit patchy. Both these sorts of hotels provide private bathrooms, mini-bars, TV, laundry service, often IDD telephone facilities and swimming pools etc. There are several restaurants to choose from, offering European as well as Chinese cuisine, and often a range of shops from bakers to hairdressers. You will have to register when you arrive, so keep your passport handy. And it is a good idea to label your luggage very clearly, as mix-ups have been known to occur. If you have any valuables with you, you can check them into the hotel safe.

The third category of hotel which visitors to the PRC are likely to stay in are the tourist hotels. These are much less glamorous, and cheaper. They are often older, too, and although clean may have rather idiosyncratic plumbing. As in the other two categories of hotel, western breakfast is available, but here it usually reflects the fact that the cooks are Chinese. There will be a service desk on each floor, but the service personnel will not necessarily speak English. There will probably be a TV in each room, and there will also be flasks of boiling water and Chinese tea in packets. Be prepared for the fact that many of these hotels do not accept credit cards.

You may often see Chinese people blowing their noses between their fingers on to the pavement. This is not considered bad manners. Spitting is also very common, although there have been campaigns against it for reasons of hygiene. Belching, especially just after a meal, is something else not considered impolite, and in fact is usually supposed to indicate a feeling of well-being.

Although most westerners visiting China will use western-style hotels, where the lavatories in their bathrooms will be similar to the sort they have at home, however, it is quite likely that they might come across Chinese-style lavatories when on sight-seeing trips or factory visits and so on, and thus details of them are included here. A Chinese lavatory consists of a porcelain trough set in the floor, over which one has to squat, feet on either side, facing the end where there is a kind of hood. In the PRC there is usually no lavatory paper (remember to take some with you) and even if there is, the Chinese often require one to throw it into a special bin after use rather than to flush it down the pan. (This may be because of the limitations of the sewage system but could also be because the Chinese in the PRC use what is euphemistically referred to as 'night-soil' as fertiliser.) As a result, these public lavatories, and sometimes even the communal ones in hotels, have a very distinctive and unpleasant smell and are not places in which to linger.

3

Money, Sightseeing Taxis & Tipping

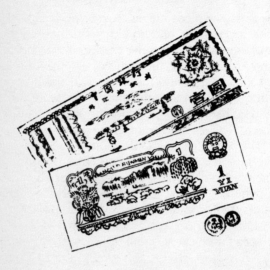

Money can also present complications in the PRC. There are two kinds of money — the ordinary currency (*renminbi*) and Foreign Exchange Certificates (FEC, or *waihui*). The latter will be given to you when you change your money at the airport or at banks and hotels. (Remember to keep enough of the receipts to cover the amount of FEC that you have in your possession when you are about to leave so that you can change it back into other currencies.)

Because Foreign Exchange Certificates are much sought-after by the local people, who have no official access to *waihui*, you will often be expected to pay for things with it, but to accept change in *renminbi*. You will not want to accumulate too much money in *renminbi*, of course, as you cannot exchange it for other currencies when you leave. So be a little cautious if accosted by the illegal 'money-changers' who are active all over China. They could get into serious trouble if apprehended, and it could be extremely embarrassing for you too.

Most sightseeing is organized by tour operators, and in the PRC can include factories as well as museums, temples, palaces and so on. On the whole, such visits are straightforward and much the same as in other countries as far as behaviour is concerned. But remember that it is polite to ask permission before you take a photograph of a person — photographers are not always welcome. In temples, be especially sensitive (there may be people worshipping) and try not to cause too much of a stir by your presence. Dress appropriately and keep your voice down.

Using taxis can present unforeseen problems. Most taxi-drivers, whether in the PRC or in Taiwan, speak no English, so it is advisable to ask someone in your hotel to write down your destination in Chinese so that you can show it to the driver. In the PRC you may occasionally find that a taxi-driver refuses to take you in his cab (for example, in the snow, because he is not insured) and one just has to be philosophical about this.

A complete contrast is afforded by a visit to the Chinese opera, usually of the Beijing (Peking) variety, which often features on the tourist itinerary. The whole spectacle is unique, and although the music might sound harsh and discordant to a western ear, the experience is another small venture into Chinese culture. Not only is what happens on stage interesting, the audience is also worth watching. They will virtually all know the story and music of the opera, and thus will feel free to get up and walk around during the performance, chat to their friends, buy snacks, and generally behave in a way quite opposite to the way an audience behaves in the West.

Tipping is not officially allowed in the PRC, and used not to occur, but in recent years, especially in the south, some service personnel have begun to make it plain that tips would not be unwelcome. In Taiwan, they are usually expected — unless stated otherwise on the bill, ten per cent is probably the norm.

4

Presents and Shopping

Tourists in the PRC are invariably pointed in the direction of the local 'Friendship Store' when they want to go shopping. These stores have a wider range of goods (usually 'typically' Chinese products like silk blouses, paintings, fans, ivory, jewellery etc.) and better-quality merchandise than most of the ordinary department stores where Chinese people do their shopping. But it is also worthwhile to investigate some of the local shops, especially when in search of something produced locally. It is not acceptable to haggle over prices in the shops, but in the free market this is perfectly all right — if one can overcome the language barrier, of course!

When you give someone a present that is wrapped, do not be surprised if the recipient thanks you for it and then puts it on one side without opening it. This is a Chinese custom and, if you think about it, dispenses with a good deal of potential awkwardness.

When Chinese visitors come to the West they invariably bring a number of small, typically Chinese presents for their hosts, and this custom is a good one to imitate. For the most senior of the people you will be dealing with, a bigger present would be in order, though if it is at all sizeable it might be a good idea to make it plain that you are giving it to him for the whole of his group or organisation. Otherwise, suitable gifts would be company pens (and refills, where needed), or company ties, ashtrays, small pieces of glass (e.g. paperweights) or Wedgwood. The interpreter would probably appreciate a book or two.

Whatever you do, avoid giving clocks or watches as presents. This is important, because in Mandarin the words for 'to give a clock' sound exactly the same as the words for 'to escort someone to their death.'

5

Conversation & Communication

Remember that in China the surname *precedes* the personal name — Zhang Hua is Mr Zhang, not Mr Hua. In addressing the Chinese people you meet, it is best to use Mr/Mrs/Miss plus their surnames: Chinese people are more formal than many westerners. ('Comrade,' by the way, seems to have lost popularity in recent years.) You may well find that many Chinese people, especially in Taiwan, have chosen English personal names for themselves, in which case they may ask you to call them by those names instead. Do not be surprised if the names chosen are not always what we might think of as suitable for personal names — surnames and tradenames are not uncommon.

You may also find that the Chinese refer to one another by their job-title — Mayor Wang, Manager Li and so on. This is a direct translation of the way they would normally refer to one another in Chinese, and you might well find it helpful if you pick up this habit, because you are almost bound to meet several people with the same surname.

Because of upheavals in the education system during the Cultural Revolution and afterwards, the amount of English which your Chinese contacts know will vary considerably. Some of them may know no English at all, but even those who do know some will almost invariably have had much less practice in speaking the language than in reading and writing it. So be patient, use short sentences, speak a little more slowly than usual if you suspect you are not being understood, and try not to use unnecessarily difficult words, or slang. Be prepared to rephrase what you have said, rather than just repeat it, and be sure not to raise your voice. In Taiwan especially, many Chinese people are more attuned to an American pronunciation than to an English one.

If you are using an interpreter, try not to say too much at a time — give him (or her) a chance to interpret a manageable amount of what you say before moving on to the next sentence. It is important to maintain eye-contact with the person you are dealing with, rather than solely with the interpreter.

Although in accounts of traditional China western writers often made the point that Chinese people were not given to being direct in conversation and favoured the oblique approach to almost all subjects, in fact you will probably find that the Chinese people you meet, while still treating you very courteously, are often more direct than many westerners. You may be asked questions about your age, marital status and salary — and you, in your turn, can ask them about the same sorts of things.

This curiosity is particularly true in the PRC, perhaps because a long period of isolation from much contact with the West has bred a great curiosity about it. It also means, of course, that the Chinese tend to seize every opportunity they can to practise their English! Do not be surprised if you are accosted in the street by young people who produce one or two sentences in English and then, overcome by embarrassment, lapse into silence. You may be the first foreigner they have ever seen, let alone spoken to.

6

Making Friends

If you are fortunate enough to have made friends with a Chinese person on an individual basis, you will soon realise that there is no concept in China of 'going Dutch.' You can offer to pay for both of you — on the bus say, or when going to the cinema — but not just for yourself. Your offer will almost certainly be refused, in which case the thing to do is offer to pay on the journey back, next time, etc. You may find that your offers are always refused, however, because the Chinese believe that they should not allow 'foreign guests' to pay for anything while they are in China.

Again, if you have Chinese friends you may be lucky enough to be invited to a Chinese home, although in the PRC it is very rare. (I am not referring here to the kind of artificial visit 'to the masses' which is included in some tours of China.) There could be several reasons for this: shortage of space is the one most often quoted, but other considerations may be distance, insecurity about having dealings with foreigners in the first place, and feelings of inferiority with regard to material possessions. It goes without saying, therefore, that one has to show great tact and consideration here, especially concerning the last two points mentioned above.

Not surprisingly, in view of past events, many Chinese in the PRC are still quite wary of being seen to consort with foreigners, and foreigners should respect this. As to the difference in personal possessions, you will notice this as soon as you enter the door: even the family's most prized items may look old-fashioned or ill-designed to a westerner so be careful about any comments you make.

In Taiwan, which is one of Asia's most rapidly prospering regions, the situation is rather different, although again it would be quite unusual for a foreigner to be invited to a Chinese home unless he or she had been in Taiwan for a while and knew the Chinese hosts well. Some homes in Taiwan are still fairly basic by western standards, but with the growth of a wealthy middle-class more and more homes are now equipped with all modern conveniences and are as comfortable as middle-class homes in the West.

Be prepared to take off your shoes in Taiwan and put on the slippers provided for you — many families have preserved this custom from the time when the island was occupied by the Japanese. Some families still live in Japanese-style homes, although in the cities at any rate these are rapidly being replaced by modern developments, and many of them have at least one room where the floor is covered with *tatami* (the thick, standard-size rush mats found so commonly in Japan). These have to be treated carefully, as they cannot really be cleaned: hence the need to remove your shoes. (Try to remember not to wear socks with holes in them!) In the PRC floors are usually made of concrete, with maybe a rug or mat on top.

7

Women Visiting China

Foreign women visiting China will have no occasion to feel ill at ease simply because they are female. There may not be equal numbers of men and women in all occupations or at all levels in China, but there are, in theory at any rate, equal opportunities for both sexes, and the Chinese are quite happy to deal with both men and women, in business or as tourists.

Women who frequently visit the PRC on business report that they are well accepted by their male Chinese counterparts and that it is not considered odd if they reciprocate toasts at banquets and so on. They should dress modestly (no sun-dresses or low-necklines, for example) and not behave in too extrovert a manner — 'loud' behaviour or flashiness in either sex does not go down well in China. In the less cosmopolitan areas of the PRC, foreigners will be stared at constantly (blondes may have their hair touched) and it is obviously not a good idea to draw even more attention to oneself by inappropriate behaviour.

Women in China often do not drink alcohol, so that if a western woman prefers to drink non-alcoholic drinks no-one will be at all surprised. Female visitors should also bear in mind that there are no western-style chemist shops in the PRC and so they will have to equip themselves with all the cosmetics, toilet articles etc. that they require before they set out from home.

8

Visiting a Doctor

If you fall ill in China, you should be able to arrange a visit to the doctor through the staff at your hotel. (In the PRC this might entail a trip to the local hospital.) It is very worrying for the Chinese, who see themselves as hosts in this situation, to have a sick foreigner on their hands, and they will make great efforts to see that you are well cared for. Standards of care do vary, however, and you would be well-advised to take with you a supply of any medicines or pharmaceutical products you think you may need, and to make sure that you have adequate insurance cover. (Medical care is not free in either Taiwan or the PRC.) You will probably be offered a choice of western-type treatment or traditional Chinese medicine (including acupuncture) for some complaints.

9

Business

Whole books have been written on doing business with China, so no mention will be made here of how to conduct negotiations. But it is worth bringing up one or two points which fall more appropriately under the rubric of etiquette. When you go to a business meeting, the first thing that happens along with the introduction is an exchange of business cards. When someone hands you his card, make sure to read it, not just glance at it and put it away. You may well find it helpful to place the cards you receive on the table in front of you, so that it is easier to remind yourself of the names of your Chinese counterparts.

It is a good idea to take along a large stock of your own cards, if possible with a Chinese version of your name and position within your company on the back. If you cannot get the cards done locally, for example, through an airline or translation agency, there are many name-card services in Hong Kong. Do try to get whoever chooses your Chinese name for you to keep it to two or three syllables — anything longer will be difficult for the Chinese to manage. And remember that in Taiwan the simplified forms of Chinese characters (now in use in the PRC) are not acceptable. Check this when you order your cards from the printer.

Dress should be quite formal — suits and ties are best, although some western businessmen do wear safari-suits, especially in hot weather.

The Chinese are very status-conscious, so it is best to remember, when dealing with a group, that they will come into the room in order of seniority. Make sure to shake hands with all of them — it is impolite to shake hands with only the first few and then give up. You will no doubt notice that there is no custom of giving precedence to the women members of the group.

When engaged in business negotiations, as in other situations, a Chinese person may feel that a direct 'no' would be embarrassing to both parties, and try to convey his disagreement by more indirect methods, such as evading the question or remaining silent. The western businessman should therefore be sensitive to this, and learn to interpret the signals which his Chinese counterpart is giving out. In some cases, of course, what appears to be an attempt at stalling may genuinely mean that the person you are dealing with has to consult with his superiors, but in other cases it may be a sign that concessions on your part are required if the discussions are to go much further.

Although much business entertaining is done in restaurants, it is not usual for spouses to be invited along. If your spouse is in China with you, she/he can expect to have to amuse herself/himself on the evening(s) when there are banquets and so on, unless specifically included in the invitation.

Punctuality is considered very important when doing business in China. The people with whom you are dealing will not keep you waiting, and you should make a point of being on time as well.

After you arrive in China, your travelling arrangements will usually be taken care of by the organization you are visiting. You will probably be met by representatives of the organization when you arrive, either at the airport or the railway station, and you will be seen off by them when you leave. More senior members of the organization are likely to say goodbye to you at your hotel, while relatively junior members will escort you all the way to your point of departure. This is the custom in China, and not a mark of any special esteem.

Once you have returned from China to your own country, it would be a nice gesture to remember your Chinese contacts the following Christmas (or, preferably, New Year) by sending them small gifts, such as calendars. This will be much appreciated.

10

Banquets and Being Entertained

In China, as already mentioned (*see* Ch.6 'Making Friends') foreigners are only rarely invited to private homes. There are many reasons for this, often very practical ones such as limited space, and the Chinese prefer to entertain in restaurants even when inviting other Chinese for a meal.

The Chinese host, who usually sits facing the door, will place the most eminent guest in the seat of honour, i.e. to his right, and the deputy Chinese host will place the next most senior guest on *his* right, at the opposite side of the table. If there is an intepreter, he will probably be seated to the right of the most important guest. Hosts and guests will usually be seated alternately round the table.

Banquets are a regular feature of life for the business person visiting China, especially if there is a group of you, and can consist of up to a dozen courses, so it is a good idea to pace yourself carefully. In the north of China, soup is often served at the end of the meal, which will usually begin with a dish of cold hors d'oeuvres. (The Chinese do not, on the whole, eat dessert, though fresh fruit may be provided — usually oranges cut into pieces.) If there is any rice, it will not be served until near the end of the meal: it is seen as a 'filler' in case the guests are still hungry, and therefore it is politic to leave some of it in your bowl, to show that you have been well fed.

When you sit down at the table, you are unlikely to find a knife and fork laid for you, so be prepared to try eating with chopsticks. (Practice in this prior to departure for China would be useful — but asking for a demonstration from your hosts can be a helpful way of breaking the ice.) And watch what the Chinese diners do when they help themselves from the communal dish of food — they may use a serving spoon, but it is also very common to use one's own chopsticks. Do not be surprised if your host is continually placing the tastiest morsels on your plate — this is one way of honouring a guest, who should always wait to be urged to eat before helping himself.

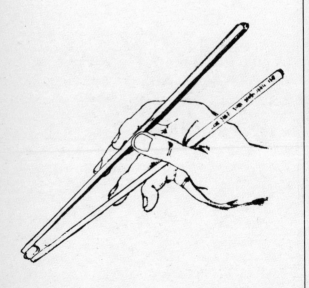

Before and/or after the meal, you may be given a hot damp towel to wipe your hands with. If it is before the meal, you can use it as a napkin for sticky fingers through the meal. If you find a bone or piece of gristle in your mouth and want to remove it, use your chopsticks or the porcelain soup spoon, *not* your fingers. The Chinese themselves would spit it out, so that too would be acceptable. As to lifting your bowl (of soup, rice etc.) towards your mouth, that is also perfectly all right.

Alcohol and Tea

Alcohol is important at banquets and formal meals. (The Chinese tend not to drink without food.) You will probably find three glasses beside your plate, one for the very good lager-type beer which is commonly drunk and is not very strong, one for some kind of wine (either of the vermouth-type or, in the PRC, one of the very sweet and syrupy grape wines produced there) and a small one for a more fiery liquor, such as *maotai*, which is distilled from sorghum and is 65-70° proof. The *maotai* is usually used for toasts and you will often see the Chinese finish off a whole glass each time.

The Chinese equivalent of 'Cheers' is *ganbei* (lit. dry glasses). (Caution is advisable here, because there are often a number of toasts. It should also be pointed out that the consumption of large amounts of alcohol at such meals is being officially discouraged.) If you do not want to drink alcohol, orange squash (fizzy) and mineral water are usually available.

Speeches, and their concluding toasts, usually happen quite soon after the beginning of the meal. The host will probably speak between the first and second courses, and the chief guest should reply a few minutes later, after the start of the second course. Take a lead from your host, keep the speech short — perhaps just a few general appreciative comments and remarks about future cooperation, friendly ties between your organizations and so on — and above all avoid elaborate jokes (often untranslatable, or at least no longer funny once they have been translated).

One other thing to remember: do not take the easy option and spend the entire time conversing with your western colleagues. This is very impolite. Talking to your Chinese hosts may seem difficult but can be very rewarding. Food is one good topic of conversation, and discussion of the relative merits of different places in China is another.

It is a good idea to arrange a return banquet for your Chinese hosts before you leave. Ask your interpreter, or whoever is organizing your visit, about this, and remember to keep time free for it. A table-plan should be drawn up, and at the banquet there should be place-cards. A supply of foreign cigarettes is always welcome on such occasions. And do remember to keep offering food to the Chinese party — Chinese people are very loath to help themselves, and will often decline something offered to them several times before accepting it, so you will have to keep pressing them to eat.

The Chinese drink large quantities of tea (no milk or sugar, of course), but this is consumed at meetings and at work, not — on the whole — in restaurants. It is usually served in mugs with lids. Cigarette smoking is widespread and cigarettes are almost always offered along with the tea.

Eating Out

Although meals are included in the overall arrangements for most people who visit China on business or as tourists, and will be taken either in the hotels they stay in or at restaurants known to one's business contacts or the tour operator, it is nevertheless interesting to venture out and eat in other restaurants. Independent travellers do this most of the time, of course, and it is a good way to experience the 'real' China. You need to be willing to communicate on your own by gestures and good humour, since you cannot expect to find anyone who speaks English (and the very arrival of a foreigner may well cause consternation in the first place), but you would be surprised how easy it is once you try.

In the PRC (and sometimes in Taiwan too), be prepared for levels of hygiene far below those of the West — the floor may be littered with chicken bones, for example — and uncertain standards of service. But more and more small, family-run restaurants are opening up in the cities of the PRC now, and food here is often good, as well as cheap, while service is usually very friendly. In Taiwan, food is no longer as astonishingly inexpensive as it was, but it is still generally of a high standard and there is more choice of cuisine within a given city.

13

Japan & Hong Kong

A word of warning about the attitude of the Chinese people to the Japanese. Although it would be denied in public, privately many Chinese people do not hesitate to admit that the Japanese are intensely disliked. This dates back to the Sino-Japanese War of 1894-5, but more especially to Japan's invasion of China in the 1930s including the occupation of Manchuria and the rape of Nanjing (Nanking) in 1937. The dislike has been fuelled recently by such things as the suspicion that the Japanese are dumping sub-standard goods on China. So it might be as well to avoid being too lavish in your praise of Japan. (This also applies to former mainlanders in Taiwan, of course, but you may find that the native Taiwanese Chinese do not share such feelings towards the Japanese, even though they were under Japanese occupation for fifty years.)

The subject of Hong Kong is not a particularly touchy one in the PRC, because the future of the colony has now been settled to China's satisfaction. Chinese people no longer hurl accusations of exploitation and imperialism at western nations in the way they once did (although when one visits museums where there are displays concerning the Opium Wars, one might feel such accusations had more than a grain of truth in them). In Taiwan, of course, the situation is rather different — the Chinese in Taiwan are closely watching everything that happens to Hong Kong in the period before the hand-over in 1997 and afterwards, in case they are next to receive the attentions of the mainland, as they have in the past.

Something about the Language: Mandarin

China is such a vast country, with obvious problems of communication, it is not surprising that several different forms of the Chinese language have developed. These are usually referred to as dialects, but since they are often mutually unintelligible it is in many cases more helpful to think of them as separate languages. They include Mandarin, Cantonese, Shanghainese, Hakka, Hokkien (Fukien) and many others. Mandarin is the language used in both the PRC and Taiwan as the medium of education and lingua franca. In the PRC it is called *putonghua* (common speech) and in Taiwan it is known as *guoyu* (national language).

This means that, in theory at any rate, everyone over fifty should be able to speak Mandarin — even if, at home, they prefer to speak their own local variety of Chinese. (Written Chinese is much the same throughout the country, though in the PRC many of the characters are now written in a simplified form.)

Chinese is a tone-language. This means that differences in the pitch at which a particular syllable is pronounced convey differences in meaning. For example, *tāng*, means 'soup' but *táng* means 'sugar'; *gǒu* means 'dog' but *gòu* means 'enough'.

There are four tones in Mandarin:
- ‾ level (and relatively high)
- ´ rising
- ˇ fall-rise
- ` falling

The marks over each syllable in the vocabulary list opposite are tone-marks. Unmarked syllables are those which are spoken so lightly as to be virtually toneless.

For most non-Chinese people the tones are the greatest obstacle to speaking Chinese correctly. They need a good deal of practice — but, as with using chopsticks, if you ask your Chinese contacts to help you improve your pronunciation, this can be a useful conversational gambit.

SIMPLE VOCABULARY

Hello (lit., you well?)	你好	nǐ hǎo?
Goodbye (lit., again see)	再见	zài jiàn
Thank you	谢谢	xiè xie
Good morning	早	zǎo
Welcome	欢迎	huānyíng
Sorry, excuse me (not used as much as in English)	对不起	duìbuqǐ
England	英国	Yīnggúo
English (person)	英国人	Yīnggúorén
English (language)	英国话, 英语	Yīnggúohuà, Yīngyǔ
America	美国	Měigúo
American (person)	美国人	Měiguórén
China	中国	Zhōnggúo
Chinese (person)	中国人	Zhōngguórén
Chinese (language)	中国话；汉语	Zhōnggúohùa; Hànyǔ (in the PRC)
Canada	加拿大	Jiānádà
Canadian	加拿大人	Jiānádàrén
Australia	澳大利亚	Aòdàlìyà
Australian	澳大利亚人	Aòdàlìyàrén
New Zealand	新西兰	Xīnxīlán
New Zealander	新西兰人	Xīnxīlánrén
I can't speak Chinese	我不会说 中国话	Wǒ bù hùi shūo Zhōnggúohùa
I am ...	我是..	wǒ shì . . .
Where is . . . ?	..在哪儿?	. . . zài nǎr?
Restaurant	饭馆儿	fànguǎnr
Hotel	旅馆	lǚgǔan
Lavatory	厕所	cèsuǒ (in the PRC)
	洗手间	xǐshǒujiān (in Taiwan)
Railway station	火车站	huǒchēzhàn
Post office	邮局	yóujú

The romanised form of Mandarin used here is called *pinyin* and is the one which is used in the PRC for text-books and so on. Foreign learners should remember that they cannot automatically give the letters their usual sounds, however. Many of the sounds in Chinese do approximate English sounds, but there are a number of conventions which should be observed:

c is pronounced as *ts* in 'cats'
z is pronounced as *ds* in 'seeds'
q is pronounced as *ch* in 'cheap'
j is pronounced as *j* in 'jig'
x is pronounced as something between *sh* in 'shin' and *s*
s as in 'siesta'
r is pronounced as a cross between *s* in 'vision' and *r* in 'red'
h is pronounced as *ch* in Scottish 'loch'
zh is pronounced as *j* in 'July'
a is like *ar* in 'far'
-ang is like *ung* in Southern English 'sung'
e is like *er* in 'her'
en is like *en* in 'stricken'
ei is like *ay* in 'hay'
ou is like *ou* in 'soul'
i is like *ee* in 'see,' except after c s z r ch sh and zh, when it is like the *i* in American 'sir'
u is like *oo* in 'soon'
ü is like *ee* in 'see' but said with the lips rounded as if for *oo*
-ong is like *ung* in German 'Jung'
-ian is like 'yen'
-ui is like 'way'

FOOTNOTE

You may have noticed that there are no words given for 'Yes,' 'No' or 'Please.' This is because there are no direct equivalents. Instead of 'Yes' you could sometimes use *dùi-le*, which really means 'correct'; instead of 'No,' you could sometimes use *bù*, but since this really means 'not' and is generally followed by the verb used in the preceding question, it does tend to sound rather blunt on its own. As for 'Please,' you will hear Chinese people using *qǐng* followed by a verb, but this literally means 'I invite you to . . .' and cannot be used, for example, when buying things in shops.

VOCAB /MEMO

VOCAB /MEMO